Today I am . . .

An Alligator

by Jane Bottomley

IDEALS CHILDREN'S BOOKS

Nashville, Tennessee

What am I going to be today?

The things in my closet
might give it away.

Today I am . . .

an alligator!

I have lots of teeth
and a great big smile.

In fact, I'm a bit
like a crocodile!

Like all alligators
with long swishy tails,

from end to end I am
covered with scales.

You had better hide
when I step outside,

and please don't make a fuss
when I catch the bus.

Don't step on my tail,
or I very well might

just give you a nip
or a friendly bite.

My jaws could go SNAP

and you'd be caught in a trap!

So you'd better watch out
when it's time for lunch;

it might just be YOU
that I'm planning to munch.

By the end of the day,
I've had a good play.

And when bedtime draws near,
it's a good thing to hear
my mommy say . . .

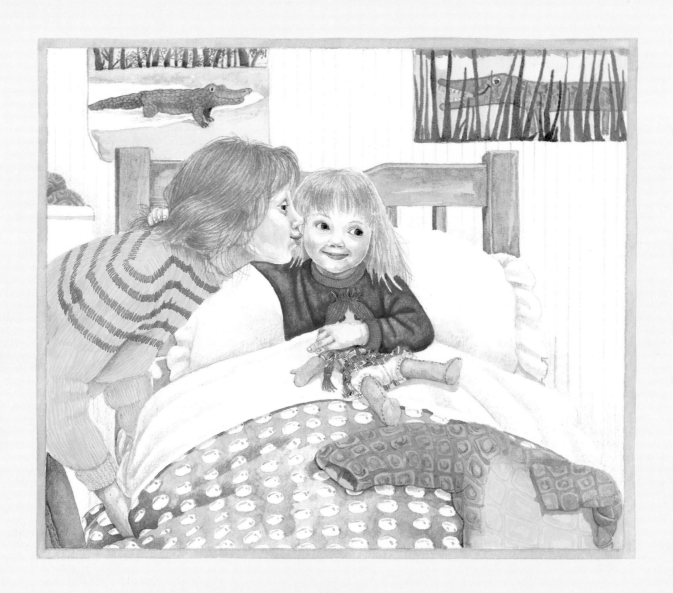

"Good night!"
and she's glad that I'm me!